# HÄGAR: THE NORD STAR

There may be some argument about which European first discovered America — an Italian or a Viking. But now the whole world has discovered that jolly Viking, Hägar the Horrible.

Hägar is back with his entire Viking crew plus Helga, Honi, Hamlet, Snert, Kvack and, of course, Lucky Eddie, Hägar's sidekick.

Here's your chance to join the more than 100 million people who "discover" and enjoy Hägar every day, in over 1600 newspapers around the world.

Hägar's creator is Dik Browne, twice winner of the Reuben Award, the National Cartoonist Society's highest honor.

*Hägar the Horrible Books*

# HÄGAR ®
## THE HORRIBLE

*by* Dik Browne

# THE NORD STAR

J

JOVE BOOKS, NEW YORK

HÄGAR THE HORRIBLE: THE NORD STAR

A Jove Book / published by arrangement with
King Features Syndicate

PRINTING HISTORY
Jove edition / November 1987

ISBN: 0-515-09259-2

Jove Books are published by The Berkley Publishing Group,
200 Madison Avenue, New York, New York 10016.
The name "JOVE" and the "J" logo
are trademarks belonging to Jove Publications, Inc.

PRINTED IN THE UNITED STATES OF AMERICA

10   9   8   7   6   5   4   3   2   1

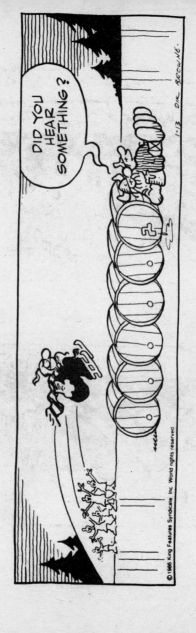

DIK BROWNE

1-23

2-3

DIK BROWNE.

HAMLET SAID I'M TOO AGGRESSIVE

HE SAID A LADY SHOULD BE MORE RESTRAINED

TODAY I'M WORKING ON MY RESTRAINT

TOMORROW I'LL PUNCH HIM

THIS CASTLE HAS GUARD TOWERS, ARMED BATTLEMENTS, BOILING OIL, A DEEP MOAT AND A DRAWBRIDGE...

3-4

AND FOR SECURITY— A 24-HOUR DOORMAN!

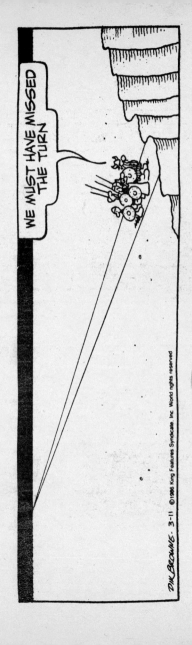